VEGAN DIET FOR SENIORS WITH CHRONIC KIDNEY DISEASE

Easy Plant-Based Recipes to Prevent, manage And Reverse Renal Disease

MALONEY DEAN

Other Books by The Same Author

VEGAN DIET COOKBOOK FOR RENAL DISEASE

VEGAN DIET MEAL PLAN FOR DIABETICS

TABLE OF CONTENTS

CHAPTER 4: SNACKS RECIPES FOR SENIORS WITH KIDNEY DISEASE

1. Hummus and Veggie Sticks:
2. Trail Mix with Nuts and Dried Fruits:
3. Kale Chips:
4. Fruit and Nut Butter Dip:
5. Roasted Chickpeas:
6. Chia Seed Pudding with Berries:
7. Rice Cake with Avocado:
8. Nut Butter Energy Bites:
9. Veggie Sushi Rolls:
10. Edamame Salad:
11. Cucumber and Hummus Bites:
12. Vegan Yogurt Parfait:
13. Rice Paper Veggie Wraps:
14. Mixed Fruit Salad with Mint:

CHAPTER 5: 7 DAY MENU PLAN

CONCLUSION

APPRECIATION

INTRODUCTION

Welcome to a journey that's all about taking charge of your health and embracing a new way of living. Imagine this: a book that's not just pages and words, but a roadmap to feeling better and living better — especially if you're a senior dealing with chronic kidney disease.

Let me introduce you to the heart of this book — a person named Evelyn. She's a true inspiration, facing the challenges of aging and kidney issues head-on.

But here's the thing: she's not letting them define her. In fact, she's showing us all how a vegan diet can be a game-changer.

See, this isn't just a story about Evelyn. It's a guide for you, showing how a plant-based diet can bring more energy, vitality, and joy to your life.

We'll talk about what to eat, what to avoid, and how to make those delicious meals that can actually help your kidneys.

This isn't about fancy words or complicated plans. It's about simple, practical steps that you can take to improve your health and well-being.

So, if you're ready to discover how a vegan diet can make a real difference for seniors dealing with kidney issues, turn the page and let's dive in together. Your journey to better health starts right here.

CHAPTER 1: VEGAN DIET
BREAKFAST RECIPES

1. Creamy Oatmeal with Mixed Berries and Almonds:

Ingredients:

1/2 cup rolled oats

1 cup unsweetened almond milk

Mixed berries (blueberries, raspberries, strawberries)

Chopped almonds

Drizzle of honey (optional)

Preparation:

Combine oats and almond milk in a saucepan. Cook over medium heat until creamy.

Serve in a bowl, top with mixed berries and chopped almonds.

Drizzle honey on top if desired.

2. Quinoa Breakfast Bowl with Apple and Cinnamon:

Ingredients:

1/2 cup cooked quinoa

Chopped apple

Chopped walnuts

Sprinkle of ground cinnamon

Preparation:

Mix cooked quinoa with chopped apple and walnuts.

Sprinkle ground cinnamon on top and mix well.

3. Avocado Toast with Tomato and Basil:

Ingredients:

1 ripe avocado

Whole grain toast

Sliced tomato

Fresh basil leaves

Balsamic vinegar

Preparation:

Mash up the avocado and spread it on the toast. Then, top it off with some sliced tomato and some fresh basil leaves.

Drizzle with balsamic vinegar.

4. Tofu and Veggie Scramble:

Ingredients:

Firm tofu, crumbled

Chopped bell peppers (various colors)

Chopped spinach

Chopped onion

Turmeric and black salt (kala namak) for seasoning

Preparation:

Sauté chopped onion and bell peppers until tender.

Add crumbled tofu and chopped spinach.

Season with turmeric and black salt for an eggy flavor.

5. Chia Seed Pudding with Mango and Almonds:

Ingredients:

3 tbsp chia seeds

1 cup almond milk

Diced mango

Sliced almonds

Drizzle of maple syrup

Preparation:

Mix chia seeds and almond milk. Leave it in the refrigerator all through the night.

In the morning, layer diced mango and sliced almonds on top.

Drizzle with maple syrup.

6. Fruit Salad Parfait with Coconut Yogurt:

Ingredients:

Mixed fruits (berries, kiwi, melon)

Coconut yogurt

Granola

Preparation:

Chop mixed fruits and layer them in a glass.

Add a layer of coconut yogurt.

Sprinkle granola on top.

7. Sweet Potato Hash with Avocado:

Ingredients:

Diced sweet potatoes

Chopped onion

Chopped bell peppers

Chopped kale

Avocado slices

Nutritional yeast

Preparation:

Sauté diced sweet potatoes, onion, and bell peppers until cooked.

Add chopped kale and cook until wilted.

Finish off the dish with some avocado slices and a dusting of nutritional yeast.

8. Green Smoothie Bowl with Fresh Fruits:

Ingredients:

Mixed berries (frozen or fresh)

Banana

Handful of spinach

Almond milk

Sliced fruits (kiwi, strawberries, banana)

Chopped nuts and seeds (e.g., almonds, chia seeds)

Preparation:

Mix together some berries, a banana, spinach, and almond milk until it's blended into a smooth consistency.

Pour into a bowl and top with sliced fruits, chopped nuts, and seeds.

9. Buckwheat Pancakes with Peach and Walnuts:

Ingredients:

1/2 cup buckwheat flour

1/2 cup almond milk

Chopped peaches

Chopped walnuts

Agave syrup

Preparation:

Mix buckwheat flour and almond milk to make pancake batter.

Cook pancakes on a griddle.

Top with chopped peaches, chopped walnuts, and a drizzle of agave syrup.

10. *Cinnamon Rice Porridge with Raisins:*

Ingredients:

1/2 cup cooked brown rice

Water or almond milk

Ground cinnamon

Raisins or chopped dates

Preparation:

Mix cooked brown rice with water or almond milk until creamy.

Sprinkle with ground cinnamon and add raisins or chopped dates.

11. Vegan Greek Yogurt Parfait with Flaxseed:

Ingredients:

Coconut or almond milk yogurt

Mixed chopped fruits

Granola

Ground flaxseed

Preparation:

Layer yogurt, mixed chopped fruits, and granola in a glass.

Sprinkle ground flaxseed on top.

12. Tofu Breakfast Burrito with Black Beans:

Ingredients:

Whole grain tortilla

Scrambled tofu

Black beans (cooked and drained)

Diced tomatoes

Avocado slices

Preparation:

Fill a tortilla with scrambled tofu, black beans, diced tomatoes, and avocado slices.

Roll up the tortilla to form a burrito.

13. *Millet Breakfast Bowl with Butternut Squash:*

Ingredients:

1/2 cup cooked millet

Sautéed spinach

Roasted butternut squash cubes

Toasted pumpkin seeds

Preparation:

Mix cooked millet with sautéed spinach and roasted butternut squash cubes.

Top with toasted pumpkin seeds.

14. Nut Butter and Banana Wrap:

Ingredients:

Whole grain tortilla

Almond or peanut butter

Sliced banana

Preparation:

Spread nut butter on a tortilla.

Place sliced banana in the center and roll up the tortilla.

These recipes offer a variety of flavors and textures while being mindful of kidney health.

CHAPTER 2: VEGAN DIET LUNCH RECIPES

1. *Lentil and Vegetable Soup:*

Ingredients:

1 cup green lentils

Chopped carrots, celery, and zucchini

Low-sodium vegetable broth

Chopped fresh parsley

Preparation:

Rinse lentils and combine with chopped vegetables in a pot.

Add enough vegetable broth to cover, and simmer until lentils are tender.

Garnish with chopped parsley before serving.

2. *Chickpea and Quinoa Salad:*

Ingredients:

Cooked quinoa

Cooked chickpeas

Chopped cucumber, bell peppers, and red onion

Chopped fresh mint

Lemon juice and olive oil dressing

Preparation:

Mix cooked quinoa, chickpeas, and chopped vegetables in a bowl.

Drizzle with lemon juice and olive oil dressing.

Add chopped fresh mint and toss well.

3. *Roasted Vegetable Wrap:*

Ingredients:

Roasted vegetables (e.g., bell peppers, eggplant, zucchini)

Whole grain wrap

Hummus

Fresh spinach leaves

Preparation:

Spread hummus on a whole grain wrap.

Add roasted vegetables and fresh spinach leaves.

Roll up the wrap and slice it in half.

4. Tofu and Veggie Stir-Fry:

Ingredients:

Cubed tofu

Sliced bell peppers, broccoli, and snap peas

Low-sodium soy sauce

Garlic and ginger

Preparation:

Fry the cubed tofu in a pan until it turns golden.

Add sliced vegetables, minced garlic, and grated ginger.

Stir in low-sodium soy sauce and cook until vegetables are tender.

5. Brown Rice and Black Bean Bowl:

Ingredients:

Cooked brown rice

Cooked black beans

Sliced avocado

Salsa

Chopped cilantro

Preparation:

Mix cooked brown rice and black beans in a bowl.

Top with sliced avocado, salsa, and chopped cilantro.

6. Mushroom and Spinach Quinoa Bowl:

Ingredients:

Cooked quinoa

Sautéed mushrooms and spinach

Toasted pine nuts

Lemon zest

Preparation:

Combine cooked quinoa, sautéed mushrooms, and spinach in a bowl.

Add a sprinkle of toasted pine nuts and a pinch of lemon zest for a zesty finish.

7. *Veggie Burger with Sweet Potato Fries:*

Ingredients:

Store-bought or homemade veggie burger patty

Whole grain bun

Baked sweet potato fries

Lettuce, tomato, and onion slices

Preparation:

Prepare the veggie burger patty as per the directions on the package.

Serve on a whole grain bun with lettuce, tomato, and onion.

Pair with baked sweet potato fries on the side.

8. Mediterranean Quinoa Salad:

Ingredients:

Cooked quinoa

Chopped cucumber, cherry tomatoes, red onion

Kalamata olives

Chopped fresh parsley and mint

Lemon juice and olive oil dressing

Preparation:

Combine cooked quinoa, chopped vegetables, and olives in a bowl.

Add chopped fresh parsley and mint.

Drizzle with lemon juice and olive oil dressing.

9. Cauliflower Rice Stir-Fry:

Ingredients:

Cauliflower rice

Sliced mixed vegetables (carrots, bell peppers, peas)

Low-sodium teriyaki sauce

Chopped green onions

Preparation:

Sauté cauliflower rice with sliced mixed vegetables.

Stir in low-sodium teriyaki sauce and cook until heated through.

Garnish with chopped green onions.

10. *Black-Eyed Pea Salad:*

Ingredients:

Cooked black-eyed peas

Chopped bell peppers, cucumber, and red onion

Chopped fresh parsley

Balsamic vinegar and olive oil dressing

Preparation:

Mix cooked black-eyed peas, chopped vegetables, and fresh parsley in a bowl.

Top off your dish with a balsamic vinegar and olive oil dressing.

11. *Veggie and Lentil Stew:*

Ingredients:

Mixed vegetables (carrots, celery, potatoes)

Cooked green or brown lentils

Low-sodium vegetable broth

Herbs (thyme, rosemary)

Salt-free seasoning blend

Preparation:

Sauté mixed vegetables in a pot until slightly softened.

Add cooked lentils, vegetable broth, herbs, and seasoning blend.

Simmer until vegetables are tender.

12.   Spinach and Chickpea Salad:

Ingredients:

Baby spinach leaves

Cooked chickpeas

Sliced red onion

Chopped roasted red peppers

Lemon-tahini dressing

Preparation:

Toss baby spinach leaves, cooked chickpeas, sliced red onion, and chopped roasted red peppers.

Drizzle with lemon-tahini dressing.

13. Stuffed Bell Peppers with Quinoa and Beans:

Ingredients:

Bell peppers, halved and seeded

Cooked quinoa and black beans mixture

Diced tomatoes

Baked until tender

Preparation:

Stuff halved bell peppers with cooked quinoa and black beans mixture.

Top with diced tomatoes and bake until peppers are tender.

14. Vegan Lentil Burger with Salad:

Ingredients:

Vegan lentil burger patty (store-bought or homemade)

Whole grain bun

Mixed green salad with lemon vinaigrette

Preparation:

Cook the vegan lentil burger patty according to package instructions.

Serve on a whole grain bun with a side of mixed green salad.

These lunch recipes offer a range of flavors while being mindful of kidney health.

CHAPTER 3: VEGAN DIET DINNER RECIPES

1. *Baked Stuffed Bell Peppers:*

Ingredients:

Bell peppers, halved and seeded

Quinoa and black bean mixture

Diced tomatoes

Baked until peppers are tender

Preparation:

Fill bell pepper halves with quinoa and black bean mixture.

Top with diced tomatoes.

Bake until peppers are tender.

2. *Veggie Stir-Fry with Tofu:*

Ingredients:

Cubed tofu

Mixed stir-fry vegetables (broccoli, carrots, bell peppers)

Low-sodium soy sauce

Garlic and ginger

Preparation:

Sauté cubed tofu until golden.

Add mixed stir-fry vegetables, minced garlic, and grated ginger.

Stir in low-sodium soy sauce and cook until vegetables are tender.

3. Zucchini Noodles with Pesto:

Ingredients:

Zucchini noodles (zoodles)

Homemade or store-bought vegan pesto

Cherry tomatoes, halved

Chopped basil

Preparation:

Sauté zucchini noodles until tender.

Toss with vegan pesto and top with cherry tomatoes and chopped basil.

4. Lentil and Vegetable Stew:

Ingredients:

Green or brown lentils

Mixed vegetables (carrots, celery, potatoes)

Low-sodium vegetable broth

Herbs (thyme, rosemary)

Salt-free seasoning blend

Preparation:

Sauté mixed vegetables until slightly softened.

Add cooked lentils, vegetable broth, herbs, and seasoning blend.

Simmer until vegetables are tender.

5. *Chickpea and Spinach Curry:*

Ingredients:

Cooked chickpeas

Chopped spinach

Coconut milk

Curry spices (turmeric, cumin, coriander)

Served with brown rice

Preparation:

Sauté cooked chickpeas and chopped spinach.

Add coconut milk and curry spices. Simmer until flavors meld.

Serve with brown rice.

6. Mushroom and Asparagus Risotto:

Ingredients:

Arborio rice

Sliced mushrooms and asparagus

Low-sodium vegetable broth

Chopped fresh parsley

Preparation:

Sauté sliced mushrooms and asparagus.

Add Arborio rice and cook until slightly translucent.

Gradually add vegetable broth, stirring until creamy.

Garnish with chopped fresh parsley.

7. Cauliflower and Chickpea Buddha Bowl:

Ingredients:

Roasted cauliflower florets

Cooked chickpeas

Quinoa or brown rice

Sliced avocado

Drizzle of tahini dressing

Preparation:

Roast cauliflower florets until golden.

Assemble a bowl with cooked chickpeas, quinoa or brown rice, and avocado slices.

Drizzle with tahini dressing.

8. *Vegan Lentil Loaf:*

Ingredients:

Cooked green or brown lentils

Chopped mixed vegetables (carrots, onions, bell peppers)

Rolled oats

Tomato sauce

Preparation:

Combine cooked lentils, chopped mixed vegetables, rolled oats, and tomato sauce.

Form into a loaf and bake until firm.

9. Portobello Mushroom Steaks:

Ingredients:

Portobello mushroom caps

Balsamic vinegar marinade

Grilled and served with roasted vegetables

Preparation:

Marinate portobello mushroom caps in balsamic vinegar.

Grill until tender and serve with roasted vegetables.

10. Cabbage and White Bean Stew:

Ingredients:

Chopped cabbage

Cooked white beans

Diced tomatoes

Low-sodium vegetable broth

Italian herbs (oregano, thyme, basil)

Preparation:

Sauté chopped cabbage until tender.

Add cooked white beans, diced tomatoes, vegetable broth, and Italian herbs.

Simmer until flavors meld.

11. Stuffed Acorn Squash:

Ingredients:

Acorn squash, halved and seeds removed

Quinoa and vegetable stuffing

Baked until squash is tender

Preparation:

Fill acorn squash halves with quinoa and vegetable stuffing.

Bake until squash is tender.

12. Vegan Lentil Chili:

Ingredients:

Cooked green or brown lentils

Chopped mixed vegetables (onion, bell peppers, carrots)

Diced tomatoes

Chili spices (cumin, chili powder, paprika)

Preparation:

Sauté chopped vegetables until softened.

Add cooked lentils, diced tomatoes, and chili spices.

Simmer until flavors meld.

13. *Spaghetti Squash Primavera:*

Ingredients:

Roasted spaghetti squash strands

Mixed sautéed vegetables (zucchini, cherry tomatoes, bell peppers)

Vegan Alfredo sauce

Preparation:

Sauté mixed vegetables until tender.

Toss with roasted spaghetti squash strands and vegan Alfredo sauce.

14. *Veggie Tofu Stir-Fry:*

Ingredients:

Cubed tofu

Sliced mixed vegetables (broccoli, carrots, snow peas)

Low-sodium stir-fry sauce

Served with brown rice

Preparation:

Sauté cubed tofu until golden.

Add sliced mixed vegetables and stir-fry sauce.

Serve with brown rice.

These dinner recipes offer a range of flavors while being mindful of kidney health.

CHAPTER 4: SNACKS RECIPES FOR SENIORS WITH KIDNEY DISEASE

1. Hummus and Veggie Sticks:

Ingredients:

Homemade or store-bought hummus

Sliced carrot, cucumber, and bell pepper sticks

Preparation:

Serve hummus with a variety of sliced veggies for dipping.

2. Trail Mix with Nuts and Dried Fruits:

Ingredients:

Mixed nuts (almonds, walnuts, cashews)

Dried fruits (raisins, apricots, cranberries)

Preparation:

Mix nuts and dried fruits for a satisfying and nutrient-rich snack.

3.   *Kale Chips:*

Ingredients:

Fresh kale leaves

Olive oil

Nutritional yeast

Preparation:

Toss kale leaves with olive oil and nutritional yeast.

Bake until crispy.

4.   *Fruit and Nut Butter Dip:*

Ingredients:

Sliced apple and pear

Almond or peanut butter

Preparation:

Dip apple and pear slices in nut butter for a sweet and savory snack.

5.   Roasted Chickpeas:

Ingredients:

Cooked and drained chickpeas

Olive oil

Spices (paprika, cumin, garlic powder)

Preparation:

Toss chickpeas with olive oil and spices.

Roast until crispy.

6.   Chia Seed Pudding with Berries:

Ingredients:

Chia seeds

Almond milk

Mixed berries

Preparation:

Mix chia seeds and almond milk. Let it set in the refrigerator.

Top with mixed berries before enjoying.

7. Rice Cake with Avocado:

Ingredients:

Rice cake

Sliced avocado

Sprinkle of salt and pepper

Preparation:

Top rice cake with sliced avocado.

Sprinkle with salt and pepper.

8. Nut Butter Energy Bites:

Ingredients:

Rolled oats

Almond or peanut butter

Chopped dates

Coconut flakes

Preparation:

Mix rolled oats, nut butter, chopped dates, and coconut flakes.

Roll into bite-sized balls.

9. *Veggie Sushi Rolls:*

Ingredients:

Nori sheets

Cooked quinoa or brown rice

Sliced cucumber, carrot, and avocado

Preparation:

Lay out a nori sheet and spread cooked quinoa or brown rice.

Add sliced veggies and roll tightly.

10. *Edamame Salad:*

Ingredients:

Cooked edamame

Chopped cucumber, red onion, and mint

Lemon juice and olive oil dressing

Preparation:

Mix cooked edamame, chopped vegetables, and chopped mint.

Drizzle with lemon juice and olive oil dressing.

11. Cucumber and Hummus Bites:

Ingredients:

Sliced cucumber rounds

Hummus

Chopped fresh dill

Preparation:

Top cucumber rounds with a dollop of hummus.
Sprinkle with chopped fresh dill.

12. Vegan Yogurt Parfait:

Ingredients:

Coconut or almond milk yogurt

Mixed berries

Granola

Preparation:

Layer yogurt, mixed berries, and granola in a glass.

13. *Rice Paper Veggie Wraps:*

Ingredients:

Rice paper wrappers
Sliced mixed veggies (bell peppers, carrots, cucumber)
Fresh herbs (mint, cilantro)

Preparation:

Soak rice paper wrappers in warm water until pliable.
Fill with sliced veggies and fresh herbs. Roll tightly.

14. Mixed Fruit Salad with Mint:

Ingredients:

Mixed chopped fruits (melon, berries, kiwi)
Chopped fresh mint
Lime juice drizzle

Preparation:

Toss mixed chopped fruits with chopped mint.

Drizzle with a bit of lime juice.

These snack recipes offer a variety of flavors while being mindful of kidney health.

CHAPTER 5: 7 DAY MENU PLAN

This menu is designed to be kidney-friendly, but it's important to consult with a healthcare professional or registered dietitian to tailor the plan to individual dietary needs and restrictions.

Day 1:

Breakfast:

Creamy Oatmeal with Mixed Berries and Almonds
Lunch:

Lentil and Vegetable Soup
Whole Grain Roll
Snack:

Nut Butter Energy Bites
Dinner:

Vegan Lentil Loaf
Steamed Green Beans
Day 2:

Breakfast:

Chia Seed Pudding with Berries
Lunch:

Chickpea and Quinoa Salad

Snack:

Hummus and Veggie Sticks

Dinner:

Zucchini Noodles with Pesto

Day 3:

Breakfast:

Fruit and Nut Butter Dip

Lunch:

Portobello Mushroom Steaks

Quinoa Salad with Lemon Vinaigrette

Snack:

Roasted Chickpeas

Dinner:

Cauliflower and Chickpea Buddha Bowl

Day 4:

Breakfast:

Avocado Toast with Tomato and Basil

Lunch:

Vegetable Stir-Fry with Tofu

Snack:

Rice Cake with Nut Butter

Dinner:

Mushroom and Asparagus Risotto

Day 5:

Breakfast:

Vegan Yogurt Parfait

Lunch:

Vegan Lentil Chili

Snack:

Mixed Nuts and Dried Fruits

Dinner:

Stuffed Acorn Squash with Quinoa and Veggies

Day 6:

Breakfast:

Buckwheat Pancakes with Peach and Walnuts

Lunch:

Spinach and Chickpea Salad

Snack:

Rice Paper Veggie Wraps

Dinner:

Cabbage and White Bean Stew

Day 7:

Breakfast:

Greek Yogurt Parfait with Flaxseed

Lunch:

Edamame Salad

Snack:

Kale Chips

Dinner:

Roasted Vegetable Wrap

Please adjust portion sizes based on individual needs and remember to stay hydrated by drinking water throughout the day.

This menu plan provides a diverse range of nutrients while being gentle on the kidneys.

Always consult with a healthcare professional or registered dietitian before making significant dietary changes, especially if managing chronic kidney disease.

CONCLUSION

In the journey of life, health is the greatest treasure we possess, and as we navigate the later years, it becomes even more valuable.

Throughout the pages of this book, we've delved into the power of a plant-based diet tailored to the unique needs of seniors with chronic kidney disease.

We've explored the remarkable ways that whole foods can nourish our bodies, strengthen our immune systems, and provide the foundation for a vibrant and fulfilling life.

Remember, this book isn't just about recipes and meal plans; it's about the promise of a brighter and healthier future.

By embracing the principles of a vegan diet, seniors with chronic kidney disease have the opportunity to take control of their well-being and embark on a path of improved vitality and resilience.

As you close this chapter and embark on your journey towards better health, keep in mind that every meal is a chance to nourish not only your body but also your spirit.

Embrace the flavors, savor the textures, and relish the joy of cooking and eating with purpose. Every choice you make in your diet is a step toward a life filled with vitality and well-being.

So, whether you're savoring a bowl of lentil soup, enjoying the crunch of kale chips, or exploring the world of vibrant plant-based flavors, know that you hold in your hands the keys to a healthier and more vibrant future.

The adventure of embracing a vegan diet for seniors with chronic kidney disease is a journey of empowerment, a celebration of life, and a commitment to your own well-being.

Thank you for taking this journey with us, and may your path be filled with delicious meals, renewed energy, and the joy of vibrant health

APPRECIATION

Thank you for embarking on this transformative journey with us through the pages of 'Vegan Diet for Seniors with Chronic Kidney Disease.'

Your commitment to your health and well-being is truly inspiring.

As you explore the nourishing world of plant-based living, remember that each choice you make has the potential to shape a healthier and more vibrant future.

May your path be filled with flavorful adventures, renewed energy, and the joy of embracing a lifestyle that honors both your body and the planet.

Here's to your health and a future filled with vitality!"

With gratitude,

MALONEY DEAN

Made in the USA
Las Vegas, NV
19 February 2024

85970198R00031